KidLit-O Presents

What's So Great About Bach?

A Biography of Johann Sebastian Bach Just for Kids!

Sam Rogers

KidLit-O Books

www.kidlito.com

© 2014. All Rights Reserved.

Table of Contents

About KidCaps

KidLit-O is an imprint of BookCaps™ that is just for kids! Each month BookCaps will be releasing several books in this exciting imprint. Visit are website or like us on Facebook to see more!

To add your name to our mailing list, visit this link: **http://www.kidlito.com/mailing-list.html**

Introduction

If you ever study music, chances are that you will end up hearing the name "Bach" somewhere along the line. The German composer is one of the most famous musicians of all time, and throughout his life he penned absolutely beautiful music that is still popular today. Johann Sebastian Bach, sometimes only referred to as J.S. Bach, or Sebastian Bach, wrote music that today is considered part of the classical genre.

Much of his music is still played and recognizable today. He was born at a time of musical fervor, when there were new advances being made in the world of music. Bach himself helped facilitate these changes; he was a musical extraordinaire, and his art has inspired people around the world. As the saying goes, music is a language that everyone speaks. Bach's influence has had no limits.

Chapter 1: Early Childhood

In Germany, during the later 1600s, there was a man named Johann Ambrosius Bach who fell in love with a beautiful woman named Maria Elisabeth Lämmerhirt. Johann Ambrosius was the esteemed town piper, which meant that he organized all of the music in town. He worked heavily with the church, coordinating what music was played during church sessions. Also during church, Johann would play the organ himself. After all, he was a hugely talented musician.

In fact, the whole Bach family was made up of talented musicians! All of Johann Ambrosius's brothers either played the organ in church, directed music, or even composed it themselves, a skill that is devilishly difficult to master. The Bach family was known for their musical talent, and so it seemed that all children born into the family must indeed have a natural aptitude.

Johann Ambrosius married Maria in 1668, on a lovely April day. Over the course of their marriage, the two of them had eight children. Unfortunately, only five of them survived, which absolutely devastated the two parents. On March 21st of 1685, the Bachs' youngest child was born, and Johann named the child after himself.

The child's full name was Johann Sebastian Bach, and little did his family know that he would go on to become one of the world's most famous and revered composers. From the time he was born, it seemed as if Johann was destined to become famous; after all, his entire family was skilled in music. His father himself played the violin, the trumpet, and the organ, along with many other instruments. Johann Sebastian would go on to do the same.

At the time, the Bach family was living in the German town of Eisenach, where his father was an organist. Also during this time period, it was expected that sons would always help their fathers with their work, and the occupation would be passed down from parent to child. Artist fathers would teach their sons to paint, and when those sons became fathers, they would teach their sons to paint. Chef fathers would teach their sons to cook, and when those sons became fathers, they would teach their sons to cook. And so it was with the Bach family, who had been musicians for generations. Not only was it encouraged, but also it was *expected*, that Johann Sebastian Bach would join the family of musicians and have a knack for music. But they never could have known that he would be a prodigy!

Since it was Johann Ambrosius's responsibility to teach Johann Sebastian all he knew about music, it is likely that he laid the foundation for a lot of his son's talent, including the violin. After all, Johann Ambrosius was especially talented at the violin, and much of Johann Sebastian's later work included string instruments. This is tremendously important to understand — Johann Sebastian Bach most likely would never have become a famous composer without his supportive and musically skilled family.

Bach's father did not have the only heavy influence on him—his uncle, Johann Cristoph Bach, taught him to play the organ. The organ is remarkably similar to a piano, but with more notes. It is often played in churches and has a distinct sound to it. Organs were immensely popular during Bach's lifetime and for years after, but they have since faded, replaced by simple pianos and keyboards. Churches, however, still retain the organ as their main musical instrument for religious services.

Only someone with extreme talent could have handled all these instruments at once. By the time Bach was eight years old, he was proficient in at least two instruments. In today's society, most children only begin to learn an instrument at eight.

But music was not the only thing that Bach had to learn. Also at the age of eight, Bach was an attendee of the Latin Grammar School. Decades ago, Latin was taught across the world as a universal language—meaning that it was *one* language that *everyone* agreed was important. While Latin is not widely spoken anymore, a lot of medical terms and biology terms are Latin.

In fact, the word *biology* comes from Latin. *Biology* is the study of life — "bio" means "life" in Latin, and "ology" means "the study of." Together, they mean "life study," or the study of life. During Bach's life, learning Latin was extremely important. Everyone spoke it!

At the Latin Grammar School, Bach was taught how to read and write. This means that he could play instruments before he could read and write! He also read the Bible extensively, in both the German and Latin language. Nearby the school, there was the church of St. Georgenkirche, and many of the schoolboys decided to create a boys' choir that would sing there. Bach leapt at the opportunity to join and, of course, he excelled. Members of the church immediately recognized his incredible voice, and people began talking about the young Bach boy who could play multiple instruments and sing better than any child they knew. The boys' choir also traveled to nearby villages, and occasionally their happy music brought joy to the troubled times, which were filled with many deaths across almost all families. Many people were ill, and sometimes children did not make it into adulthood.

Bach himself experienced numerous family deaths, which devastated him. Before the age of nine, he had lost two siblings, one sister and one brother. When he finally reached nine years old, his mother María passed away. This took an especially hard toll on the Bach family, especially Bach's father. Johann Ambrosius mourned for the loss of his wife, but he remarried fairly quickly. Within three months, he had a new wife, and Bach had a stepmother. For a small while, it seemed as if they would have a family again.

However, this idea did not hang around for long. Eight months after María died, so too did Johann Ambrosius. Bach was now ten years old, with no parents to support him. He did not want to stay with his stepmother, and neither did any of his remaining siblings.

Once of Bach's brothers, Johann Cristoph, had recently moved away from Eisenach and into a quaint town called Ohrdruf. It rested thirty miles away from Eisenach. Bach and one of his brothers, Johann Jakob, decided they would go live with Johann Cristoph. If they were going to remain a family, they needed to be together.

Chapter 2: Wandering the World

Like all of the Bach children, Johann Cristoph, the eldest brother who lived in Ohrdruf, was talented in music. He had just gotten married, and now supported five children, his wife, and his two brothers who came to live with him. Bach and Johann Jakob were incredibly thankful for his generosity, and Johann Cristoph was glad to have them.

Johann Cristoph, equally saddened by the death of his parents, knew that it could be up to him to improve Bach's music experience. So he got right down to work, teaching Bach about different composers, their musical pieces, and various instruments. Mostly, Bach studied the organ and the harpsichord. The *harpsichord* is another instrument similar in stature to a piano and an organ.

So that he could learn music, Johann Cristoph encouraged Bach to look at complicated music and copy it onto a new piece of paper. By doing this, Bach would have to painstakingly draw each note and study it, learning the music piece-by-piece, note-by-note. While this may seem overly tedious today, it was quite common during Bach's time period. This was the way that children taught themselves music.

But, like in Eisenach, music was not the only education that swelled Bach's brain. Since he was still young, he needed to attend school. While before he only learned the German and Latin languages, he added Greek to his inventory and soon became proficient. He continued his studies in theology, the study of religion. As before, "ology" means "the study of" and "theo" means "relating to a god or gods." At this school, which was called the Gymnasium, Bach was a part of the school choir, and he loved it!

When a choir sings, each person is selected for one of four parts.

The first part is called the *bass* (pronounced like *base*); this part has the lowest notes, is typically sung by men (since their voices can go deeper), and it provides a support for a song. If a choir were a concert band, the tuba would play the bass parts.

The second part is called the *tenor*; this part is a bit higher than the bass, but still on the lower side. Once again, the tenor parts are typically sung by men, but not always. It all depends on how low your voice can go. If a choir were a concert band, instruments like the tenor saxophone, the trombone, and the English horn would play the tenor parts.

The third part is called the *alto*; it is a step higher than tenor, so these parts will not go so low. More women are seen singing the alto parts, but it possible for men to sing these parts, as well. If a choir were a concert band, the viola, the French horn, and the alto saxophone would play the alto parts.

The fourth and final part is the *soprano*, which is the highest of all four parts. This does not mean that it is the most important, but it will have the highest notes. Females most commonly sing soprano parts but then again, not always. If a choir were a concert band, the soprano parts would be played by clarinets, flutes, trumpets, and soprano saxophones.

Can you guess which part Bach sang? He sang soprano! He was exceptionally talented at reaching high notes, and his teacher recognized his talent immediately. His teacher's name was Elias Herda, and he was impressed with Bach as any teacher would be. He knew that this choir in Ohrdruf was no place for a boy so talented. Instead, he wanted to send Bach to a town called Lüneburg, which had a choir that was renowned across the country.

Lüneberg was home to a monastery, whose choir supported talented young musicians who were too poor to support themselves. With no parents and a brother who was supporting seven people, this seemed like an ideal place for Bach. Elias Herda seemed to think so, especially because he had attended the monastery's choir himself when he was younger.

And so Bach set out for the town of Lüneburg—but he was not alone. One of his friends, named Georg Erdmann, was also going to sing in the monastery's choir. The journey was an incredible distance of one hundred and eighty miles. Some historians say that Bach and Erdmann walked the whole way, and others say they used carriages to get there, stopping occasionally at friendly monasteries to receive food and shelter. However, they got there, Bach and Erdmann finally arrived, and new part of Bach's life was about to begin.

Of course, the choir and the teachers in Lüneburg were incredibly impressed with Bach's voice and his motivation. He had many more concerts and performances than he had ever had back home, and he loved it! He loved performing for people; he loved singing, and he most definitely adored music. At the monastery, he began to study more advanced music, mostly German. Some of the pieces had been written by the most famous composers of all time, others were brand new and still gaining fame.

Johann Sebastian Bach was still young when he sang in the choirs with his soprano voice, and historians believe that, because he was young, his voice was higher and he was able to reach those notes. As he grew up into his teenage years, however, Bach's voice deepened, and his ability to sing soprano notes soon left him. Unable to sing those parts anymore, he decided to direct his attention toward playing instruments. If he could not sing the parts he wanted, he could at least play the violin and the harpsichord.

Performances were not the only thing on Bach's schedule in Lüneburg. When he studied in the library, he became particularly interested in classical music from France. How did he become introduced to French music? Well, one of his performances had taken place in the court of Celle Castle, approximately fifty miles to the south. Celle Castle looked like a typical German castle on the outside, but on the inside it was filled with French decorations. People often compared it to Versailles, a popular French city. Celle Castle was often home to French musicians, and Bach was proud and excited to play in such an esteemed place. When he returned to Lüneburg after his performance, he thought he might like to study more French music. This was noteworthy because it expanded Bach's library and his knowledge. A great musician cannot study pieces from one country; there are musical gems to be found around the world, and France is one of those places.

At Lüneburg, a man approached Bach. His name was Georg Böhm, a famous organist in town. He had known Bach's parents and had been a close family friend. Böhm complimented Bach on how talented and experienced he was; he also told Bach about the city of Hamburg, and taught him how they played the organ there. Bach loved hearing about other places and learning new things, and this was one of the reasons he became so well versed in music.

Johann Sebastian Bach had so far spent two years in Lüneburg. His time there was coming to a close, he knew, and he wanted to go elsewhere. But where? He could return home, where a new organist was needed. He could travel to the city of Arnstadt, where the local church also needed an organist. He decided to journey south and see where life would take him.

Bach first stopped in the town of Weimar, because Arnstadt was not yet done with building their organ. In Weimar, he played the violin in an orchestra directed by the duke's brother. While in Lüneburg, he had extensively studied French music, it was in Weimar that he studied Italian music. By this time in his life, Bach was about eighteen years old and had more musical experience than most people his age. Weimar was just a brief pit stop in his travels, however; he was now onto Arnstadt, to play a newly built, beautiful organ!

Johann Sebastian Bach stayed in Arnstadt for four years, and these were some of the most pivotal years of his life. In the town of Arnstadt, there is a replica of his organ. While the organ is a reconstruction, tourists can see the actual manual that came with it. The church encouraged Bach to temporarily leave Arnstadt, so that he might travel the country and learn some new techniques. Bach immediately agreed and visited the cities of Lübeck, Hamburg, and Lüneburg again. Upon his return, his knowledge of music had increased so much that his musical colleagues thought he was a little crazy!

Bach wanted to try new things with music; he wanted to be innovative and pen things that had never been written before. The church was upset with him; not only did his journey take three months longer than expected, but many of the church singers could not understand his new and unique way of playing the organ. Bach introduced new melodies and played in a confusing manner never heard before. The church did not want to punish Bach, because he was such a brilliant organist, but what were they to do? There were rumors spreading that Bach was bringing a special lady (a possible girlfriend) into the church, and Bach began getting temperamental, occasionally refusing to play.

That was, unfortunately, the end of his stay in Arnstadt.

But there are plenty of cities in Germany, and music was all the rage, so there was no end of opportunities for Bach. He traveled to the town of Mühlhausen, where he would soon be married.

During this time period, it was common for people to marry their cousins. Today, that is frowned upon in most cultures, but many famous historical figures did it, Bach included. He married his cousin Maria Barbara, who was also a talented musician. He was very content in his marriage, and he enjoyed Mühlhausen. He also did much of his first composing here, and he decided he wanted to renovate the rundown church facilities. If he was going to play the organ here, he was going to play in a nice building.

But, of course, trouble struck. Johann Sebastian's boss was a *Pietist*, which means he was strictly religious. In Bach's age, many of the strictly religious elders did not believe in fun, music, games, or anything that was not done for basic survival or worship to God. This meant that music was not allowed, something that Bach could not even begin to comprehend. The Bach family was clearly not a family of Pietists, but if his boss was, what could he do? His time in Mühlhausen was over, and Bach was forced to relocate once again.

He was in his young twenties now, and he had moved from town to town to town. Where was there to go next?

Toccata and Fugue in D Minor and *Jesu*

Before we learn what happened next to Johann Sebastian Bach, let us explore one of his songs written around this time period. You may have read that title, tilted your head, and said, "Huh?" *Tocatta and Fugue in D Minor* is arguably one of Bach's most famous pieces. You may not recognize the title, but you will certainly recognize the music. It is often associated with horror scenes (most often in cartoons), and is typically played on the organ. If you have ever seen Disney's *Fantasia* (1940), you heard *Tocatta and Fugue in D Minor*. It is known for its dark and frightening melody, but when you listen to it closely, it is actually quite beautiful and intelligent.

Let's break down the title. *Tocatta* is an Italian word that means "to touch." A song that is a *toccata* means that is features heavy keyboard, piano, organ, or any other similar instruments. The *toccata* is the first part of the song, characterized by quick and fast notes that take much skill to perform. It was seen as an introduction to the *fugue.*

The *fugue* is the second part of the piece; something usually comes before a *fugue*, to introduce it (in this case, the *toccata*). Some people claim that the fugue of *Tocatta and Fugue in D Minor* is the best known and best produced fugue in history—and that's saying something!

D Minor is they key in which the song was written. Songs are written in different *keys*, and a key just lets the musician know which notes they should or should not play.

Another of Johann Sebastian Bach's most famous pieces is called *Jesu, Joy of Man's Desiring.* Again, you may not immediately recognize the title, but if you spent any significant deal of time inside a church, you have likely heard the tune. It is one of the most widely played tunes in any church, and for good reason. It is a cheerful tune played on an organ, a standard instrument in most churches. A choir can also join the organ, which is also common.

Like many of the songs that Bach penned, *Jesu, Joy of Man's Desiring* has a bass, tenor, alto, and soprano line. This made the song appealing to listen to inside a church. As suggested by the title, *Jesu* stands for *Jesus,* and the song is praising God. The song's message is that it is man's desire to be closer to God, an idea that was held by many religious people in Bach's age, and is still held today.

Chapter 3: Bach on the Rise

Five years ago, while he waited for an organ to be completed at Arnstadt, Johann Sebastian Bach had stayed in the quiet little town of Weimar, and it was to this town that he returned. He never expected to return; it was small, with only a few thousand citizens, and it was not exactly a center for music. Many people had started hearing about the Bach boy who was growing up to be one of the most talented and unique musicians of the century—and he choice to return to Weimar? It was surprising.

While Weimar was not a center for music, Bach did find peace here. He continued to play the organ for the duke's court, and he played the violin, as well. He enjoyed playing for the chamber orchestra, which was composed of twenty-two talented musicians. Bach started to compose music, and he even did some arranging.

There is a difference between *composing* and *arranging* music.

To *arrange* music is to take someone else's song, and change it. You need permission from the composer, of course. Sometimes people want to make a song shorter, or write parts for more instruments, or make medleys (songs with multiple different songs in them). For example, the song "Mars: The Bringer of War" by Gustav Holst was originally written for strings and horns. However, some people want marching bands to play it, and marching bands have some different instruments than concert bands. In that case, an *arranger* would *rearrange* the music to fit their needs.

To *compose* is to create. It means to write your own music from scratch, to think up your own melodies and harmonies, choose notes that sound well together, decide which instruments play, and so on. It is often much harder to compose than arrange, and people applauded many of Bach's compositions. He was a true genius!

For six, years, he was quite content playing at the duke's court, in the chamber orchestra, and composing his own songs. He was slowly becoming famous across Weimar! In 1714, however, something special happened to Bach, something he had always dreamed of! He became the orchestra's leader, and he was to lead them in music. Everyone thought that Bach would do a fantastic job, considering how talented he was.

It was all uphill from there. Young music students began appearing in Weimar, asking to see Johann Sebastian Bach, whom they had heard of near and far. They wanted him to play in their churches and fix their organs; after all, he was the most famous organist in all of Germany! Bach was more than happy to help out. The Kapellmeister, his boss, supported him. Bach was in charge of the orchestra, but the Kapellmeister was in charge of Bach.

Nine years after Bach arrived in Weimar, a family feud started. In this time period, it was common for families to be "at war" with each other. Some feuds were violent, others were not. For example, in *Romeo and Juliet*, the two protagonists are from warring families. The Duke of Weimar, for whom Bach often played, initiated a feud with his nephew. This became extremely awkward for Bach and many of the people that served the duke's family because anyone who associated with the duke was no longer allowed to associate with the duke's nephew. Bach found the situation uncomfortable, and wished to leave almost immediately.

But before he could, he was slighted. Since Bach was second-in-command to the Kapellmeister, it seemed within reason that Bach would inherit his position, that *he* would become the Kapellmeister upon the Kapellmeister's death. However, that was not so. Instead, the Kapellmeister's son received the position.

Bach obviously felt insulted. He was a rising star in Weimar! Shouldn't he have been selected as the new Kapellmeister? A very unlikely ally came to Bach's aid, someone that he was supposed to have no contact with the duke's nephew.

The duke's nephew, still at war with his uncle, had heard of what happened to Bach, and he wanted to help. He knew that in a nearby castle, Anhalt-Cöthen, a new Kapellmeister was needed, and Bach eagerly accepted the position! However, this came at a great consequence. Bach was not supposed to talk with the duke's nephew, and he had just angered the duke, the most powerful man in all of Weimar.

When the duke heard that Bach was accepting help from his nephew, Bach was immediately arrested and thrown into jail. Bach thought this was unfair, especially since he was planning on leaving Weimar! He was not in jail for long, however. The duke ordered that Bach was to be released from jail after one month, and immediately dispatched from his position.

As soon as he was out of his jail cell, he was ready to leave Weimar, and for good. He would no longer be tangled up in the silly feuds. It was to Anhalt-Cöthen that he was no destined.

As he had always dreamed of, Bach became a Kapellmeister. It was a dream come true! He served at the Anhalt-Cöthen court, where the prince Leopold enjoyed his music. Prince Leopold was not a Pietist, the group of people who did not like music in church services, but he was a Calvinist, and they had much the same idea. At church in Anhalt-Cöthen, music was prohibited. It was seen as an unnecessary way to pay tribute to God. So, what did Bach exactly do in his role of Kapellmeister, if not play at church services?

Well, Prince Leopold was not as strict as the Pietists. He still loved hearing music outside of church, and he had heard that Johann Sebastian Bach was the most famous organist in all of Germany. He was a man who kept up with the latest trends in music; and, as Bach was breaking most of those trends and creating new ones, Prince Leopold was mightily pleased. He gathered an orchestra for Bach to lead, some of the members coming from as far away as Berlin, Germany's capital.

But Prince Leopold did far more than just listen to Bach and the court orchestra. He would sometimes even play with them! Prince Leopold played the harpsichord and the violin, just like Bach, and he often asked Bach for advice. After all, if you played music and you had a musical celebrity serving in your house, wouldn't you ask them for advice often? Bach and Prince Leopold became fast friends.

Bach still composed music during his days in Cöthen, and much of it was happy, joyous music. Oftentimes, by looking at the mood and tone of a composer's work, you can tell how happy or sad they were during that time period. If a composer writes slow, sad music, then their days were probably not full of laughter and joy. In the same manner, if an artist paints with many dark colors and tries to send foreboding messages, well, maybe the artist is not too happy. The best way to learn more about an artist or musician, sometimes, is to see what they worked on during their lifetime.

Some of Bach's most-loved works were written during his time as Kapellmeister in Anhalt-Cöthen. One series of them was called the Brandenburg Concertos, given to the leader of a placed called Brandenburg. During this time in Bach's life, he was very happy and satisfied with his job, so the music tended to be on the lighter and happier side. The Brandenburg Concertos are a perfect example of the contrasts in music during the Baroque Period. The songs had solos in them, as well as perfect arrangements for all of the other musicians. It was the perfect blend, and people loved it!

There are six concertos in all, and they all featured solos. There were solos for the following instruments: violins, oboes, bassoons, horns (trumpets or other brass instruments), and the recorder. Many people refer to each of the Brandenburg songs as a *concerto grosso*. Here, *concerto* obviously means *concert*, and *gross* means *large.* This did not mean that the concert was of an extraordinary size; in fact, the group of musicians was uncommonly small. However, the number of soloists far outnumbered what was typical for the time, and this is what people admired about the concertos. It was strange to see such a balance of soloists and ensemble players.

One of the songs that Bach wrote for Prince Leopold was titled "Air on a G String," the "G String" being one of the strings on a violin or other string instrument. We know that Bach wrote it between the years 1717 and 1723, between Bach's age of thirty-two and thirty-eight. It was not called "Air on a G String" at the time, but instead earned the name in the late 1800s.

A musician named August Wilhelm decided to play the piece, and managed to perform it using only the G-string on a violin. Bach's famous piece then received its new name, with "air" meaning "song."

Staying with Prince Leopold gave Bach an excellent opportunity to travel. Since the prince needed to see other royalty in other cities, he wanted his talented and professional group of musicians to accompany him. Unfortunately, Bach was unable to bring his wife, Maria Barbara, with him on these journeys, and he also was unable to bring any of his four children.

Upon one of his returns, he received horrible news. His wife, Maria Barbara, had died. Bach had been on the road for months, but she had suddenly caught an illness. While Bach was away, she was buried, as well. He was absolutely devastated, along with his four children.

Despite the hardships, however, life at Cöthen had to go on. Bach worked for a prince, after all, and the prince needed attending.

One year, with Prince Leopold's birthday approaching (and New Year's Eve so close to it), the court asked Bach to write some songs commemorating the celebrations. He was told that there would be singers performing these pieces, so he would have to compose them accordingly.

During the practice sessions, Bach met the singers. One of them was named Anna Magdalena, and she lived in a nearby court. She sang in a soprano voice, and when Bach heard her, he was absolutely blown away. It was love at first sound!

Bach and Anna immediately fell in love. He was thirty-six years old, and she was twenty. Also in Bach's time, it was common for people of such differing ages to marry.

Anna Magdalena knew that Bach had four children, and she eagerly wanted to take care of them. She helped around the Bach household, and even assisted Bach when he needed help composing. She was beautiful, talented, and the perfect wife for Bach!

Even Prince Leopold soon got married! He married his cousin, Friederica Henrietta von Anhalt-Bernburg. She was not such a tremendous fan of music, however, and she did not like Johann Sebastian Bach. She wanted him to leave.

At Prince Leopold's suggestion, Bach began desperately seeking a new job. After all, he had growing children to care for. He needed his paycheck! After talking to numerous people about numerous job positions, he finally found a place that suited him: a city called Leipzig, and it was to Leipzig that Bach and his family moved. He did not wish to move, because he had such an excellent friendship with Prince Leopold, but there was nothing either of them could do.

Chapter 4: "If It's Not Baroque, Don't Fix It"

When historians look at a timeline, they like to divide it up. Different time periods experience different movements and situations. For example, some people refer to art made in the 1800s as art produced during the realist period. The same rule applies to music. Johann Sebastian Bach composed and arranged music during a famous time known as the "Baroque Period," pronounced *bah – roak*. People who lived during the Baroque Period did not call it that, however; this term was not used until the 1800s.

The Baroque Period took place roughly from the start of the seventeenth century, the year 1600, to the year 1750. But where does this term come from? What exactly does Baroque even mean? Well, people got it from the Portuguese word *barroco*. *Barroco* means "extravagant." You can probably guess why this word fit pretty well with the time period. Musicians like Johann Sebastian Bach were inventing new musical styles and trying out new techniques.

From the year 500 to approximately 1500, Europe had been lodged in an era called the Dark Ages, also known as the Middle Ages. This is the era that people typically refer to when they think of kings and knights and queens and princesses and horses and battles. It was a terribly long period of war, bloodshed, illiteracy, and poverty. However, it was not to last forever. After hundreds of years of darkness, light began to shine in what became known as the Renaissance.

The word "Renaissance" means "rebirth," and that is because, right after the Dark Ages, people were once again making advances in art, literature, science, and so on. The world was pulling out of the dark ages and entering a brilliant era of thought. Music was a huge part of the Renaissance, and huge strides were made. Most of the music in Europe during this time period was produced in the name of God: for churches, sermons, funerals, or just for the sake of a tribute to the Christian religion.

The Renaissance period for music lasted for one hundred and twenty-five years, from 1475 to 1600. Johann Sebastian Bach was born eighty-five years after the start of the Baroque Period, and it ended the year he died. Thus began the classical period.

But there are many different aspects to study about the Baroque Period. For one, what did the musician during this time believe? Why did they write music in the first place? What was Bach trying to do with his music?

The musicians of Ancient Greece and Ancient Rome knew that music was more than just a few sounds in the air. Music can convey emotion; it can make you feel sad or happy, it can make you laugh or cry; it can tell a story. Today, in church and even in movies and television, music is a very powerful tool. After the shadow of the Dark Ages, musicians such as Bach once again realized the power of music. They wanted their songs to send messages. Bach wrote many songs about God and heaven since his audiences were people that went to church.

So, now that we know what Bach wanted to *do* with his music, we need to know *why his* music was so remarkable. What were some of the odd techniques and new styles that he introduced in his songs?

Firstly, the ideas of *melodies* and *harmonies* were introduced. In a piece of music, the *melody* is the main theme. It's probably what you hum to yourself if you remember a song. However, what you might not notice when you listen to music in the harmony. The harmony does not have the main part, but instead it *complements* the melody. It makes the melody's notes sound more full. Before the Baroque Period, music could be quite bland. However, melodies and harmonies combined together here and made excellent sounds.

As described before, much of the music during this period had bass, tenor, alto, and soprano parts. This was a new innovation, and people loved it! It allowed for more diversity within the music.

Also, music got exciting. Many people like music because there is *contrast*. This means that the music changes from loud to soft, from soft to loud, different instruments play at different times and then all together, and there were varying articulations (some notes were played long and slow, others were played short and quick). In the 1960s, people were astounded by the rock-and-roll style of Elvis Presley and the Beatles; similarly, during the Baroque Period, people were strangely impressed and confused over the advances in classical and church music. It was certainly a time to be alive! Music would not be the same today without changes made by Bach and his musical colleagues.

New instruments were introduced into chamber orchestras and other musical ensembles. Harpsichords became more popular, and Johann Sebastian Bach was a big fan of those. The fortepiano developed from the organ, and years later, the piano would develop from the fortepiano.

Chapter 5: Years in Leipzig

Weimar and Anhalt-Cöthen were both pretty small when compared with the city of Leipzig, which had thirty thousand people living within its boundaries. One of the reasons Bach liked this city so much is because it had a school with a good reputation, and he wanted his children to go a good school and get the best education possible. Leipzig was also the center of a lot of trade, which means there was plenty of money to go around. Bach should have no problem finding a job!

Bach was to be both the Kapellmeister in Leipzig and the Director of Choir and Music. His arrival in Leipzig was a big deal; for six months, there had been no Kapellmeister and a number of inadequate musicians had come for the job. They knew they would have no trouble with Bach if his reputation were any indication.

Not only was he to work with the church, but he was also to work at the school of St. Thomas, which hosted sixty musical students. Like the monastery at which he had studied, many of these students were incredibly talented, but were mostly too poor to afford a proper education. Bach had a special place in his heart for students like this, especially since he had once been in their place. The students would perform in churches and at funerals, an honored position.

In some schools today, but more often during Bach's age, the teachers had to live on the school campus. That way, they would always be readily available to answer students' questions, and they would never be late for work. Bach enjoyed living on the campus, though. He had an excellent view from his window, and there was enough space to accommodate his wife Anna, and their four children.

The school itself was in a great location. It was in a beautiful part of Germany, with mountains and valleys. Near the school were popular coffee shops and cafes, and there was music galore to be heard around every corner. A small river meandered nearby. Indeed, Leipzig was not only a popular destination for traders and tourists, but also a truly happy place to live.

Johann Sebastian Bach found himself almost entirely in charge of music in a school that, while in a very excellent part of journey, was falling apart. The building was not in the greatest shape, the staff members and teachers were rude and liked to bicker amongst themselves, and unsanitary conditions led to sickness sweeping through the student population. With these problems standing before him, Bach took control of four church's music programs, as well as the school's. These churches needed choirs, and his students would be the ones to make them. He was also put in charge of the church orchestra, so he needed to teach students instruments as well as singing.

At a school that was supposed to host some of the brightest musical minds in Germany, Bach was barely impressed. He said that less than half of his students were capable of even learning what he had to teach. Like a drill instructor, it was his job to take a group of inexperienced students and turn them into something else.

Practice was essential. Bach wanted the students to practice as much as they possibly could; they would be performing for church services. They could not mess up at all! The students had some "dress rehearsals" at places like coffee shops and other places around the town. The people of Leipzig were massive fans of music, and Bach was determined to succeed.

At church on Sundays, the students played a twenty-minute *cantata*. A cantata is a type of song that involves both singers and instrumentalists. The song is broken up into different sections, otherwise known as a *movement*. Cantatas are typically religious in nature as most of the songs at church are. The cantata was played before the church sermon, so citizens of Leipzig could listen to it as they shuffled into the pews of the church.

Another part of Bach's daily job was to compose religious music for the church at Leipzig's local university. He did this for approximately eleven weeks until he encountered a problem. The university told Bach that they did not want him to take charge of the university church music, and that instead the position would be given to another organist. Bach took this as an insult to his talent and his reputation, and he went immediately to a high official to complain, but to no avail.

One of the people to whom Bach reported was called the Elector of Saxony. This is about the equivalent of governor—the elector just ran part of Germany, until he became the King of Poland in 1697. This caused more problems than you might think. There are many branches of Christianity, with small variations between each one. Many people in Germans followed Lutheranism while the Polish were Roman Catholic (they support the Pope in Vatican City). When the Elector set the Polish crown onto his head, he also accepted that he was now Roman Catholic.

For the Elector's wife (and for many people in Germany, including Bach), this caused problems. For one, the Elector's wife decided to leave her husband because she thought that her husband was betraying his true religion. The people of Germany loved the Elector's wife, so this was a sad time. Many people hoped that the Elector would give up his crown for his wife, or that his wife would accept him, even if he were Roman Catholic. Neither of those things happened, however; instead, the Elector's wife died an early death.

The people of Germany were profoundly saddened by this, as was the Elector. Many people wanted to offer kind tributes to the lost noblewoman, and one of them stood out in particular. His name was Hans von Kirchbach, and he asked Bach to write a sad song in memory of the Elector's wife, to be played at Leipzig's university. Bach immediately set out to do this, but he was quickly stopped. Because he did not work for the university church, he should not have been allowed to write the music. This opened old wounds since Bach was still angry about having been denied the position at the university church.

Eventually, because of all the confusion and because Bach had already started writing, he was allowed to write the music for the Elector's wife. However, the university warned him that he was no longer allowed to write music for anything that had to do with the university — this was the final straw. The ceremony for the Elector's wife was lovely, however, and many people complimented Bach on his marvellous composition. As he wrote more music, he steadily became more popular. The King of Poland / Elector appreciated Bach's efforts, and made him the official court musician. The King of Poland lived in a castle in the German city of Dresden, and it was now for the Dresden court that Bach wrote many songs.

As you can probably believe, Bach found his hands full. He had the school to take care of. He needed to arrange musical performances around the city. He was now the official music composed for the King of Poland and the Elector of Saxony. He was revered across the country and contacted by people everywhere to write songs and build organs. Because he was so busy, he instructed one of his friends, whose name was Petzold, to take control of his classes at the school. However, the school soon found out, and they were not very happy with him. Bach was angry with them, too, however; he was only trying to make sure the students had a teacher since he was too busy. Bach was so mad that he wanted to leave Leipzig as he had left every other city.

Luckily for Bach, however, the school had just gained a new headmaster: one of his old friends, Gesner. Gesner immediately convinced Bach to stay, and he urged the officials at the school to reach a compromise with Bach. Unfortunately, Gesner did not stay at the school for long, and he was replaced with a younger man who was not a fan of the musical arts. For this reason, he and Bach quickly butted heads, and Bach wanted nothing more than to leave again.

However, as had often happened with Bach, just when one door closed, another seemed to open. In Leipzig, there was an organization called the Collegia Musica, and they were seeking a new director, after their old one moved to another city. The Collegia Musica often had concerts all around Leipzig, and Bach had long admired them and pictured himself directing them. In the year 1729, at the age of forty-four, Bach tool over the Collegia Musica as their director.

Once he became the director, he also immediately earned a friendship with a man named Gottfried Zimmerman. Zimmerman owned land in Leipzig, mainly for coffee shops, and it was common for the Collegia Musica to perform in Zimmerman's establishments. The group performed once a week in the evening, during which the people of Leipzig would happily sip their coffee and listen to music. Having Bach as a composer and a director for the Collegia Musica was an honor, and even more people realized quite how talented he was.

Bach was incredibly happy working with the Collegia Musica. At the school, the buildings were rundown, and the conditions were not the greatest. Zimmerman, however, had more money in his pockets, and he was willing to purchase new musical instruments, for a better sound quality. The new instruments were so popular, not only among the orchestra, but among the citizens too that some people just liked to look at them. As you can probably imagine, Bach was in heaven.

Bach juggled the Collegia Musica and playing for the King of Poland, who he would often visit with his son.

In Bach's age, living over fifty was sometimes uncommon. Disease and unsanitary conditions led to early deaths. Today, fifty is seen as a common age, and the average life expectancy is around seventy-five to eighty years old. This number rises with each year because we have more technology and medicine to keep people alive. Bach is lucky to have passed fifty years old, and he began feeling the effects of old age.

His old age, however, did not stop his love for music and his skills. In fact, some people say that he wrote his best music in his later years. People loved to visit him; they wanted to see the official musician for the King of Poland, the man who had brought a new love for music to the St. Thomas school, the man who had taken the reins of the Collegia Musica, bringing entertainment and happiness to people everywhere.

During these later years, he wrote some pieces that are, to this day, some of these difficult, terrifying, and rewarding pieces to play. They are called the Goldberg Variations. A *variation* is music is when the melody is repeated, but in different ways. The melody could be repeated with a different rhythm, in a harmony, with a counter-rhythm, and so on. They are often difficult to play because they sound differently than how we expect them to.

There was a Russian count, Count Kaiserling, who often stopped in Leipzig. There, he would rest on his business trips. However, he suffered from a condition called insomnia, which made it almost impossible for him to fall asleep. During his sleepless nights in Leipzig, he loved to listen to music, and he requested that Bach compose him some music for a man named Goldberg to play for him. He specified that he wanted the music to be played by a "clavier" instrument, a fancy word for a keyboard instrument (fortepiano, organ, and so on). Count Kaiserling wanted the music to be soothing, yet cheerful, and the Goldberg Variations are just that. Johann Sebastian Bach was well paid for the Variations, receiving one hundred gold coins, presented in a cup of gold. It was certainly excellent payment!

There are thirty Variations, and videos of them can be found on online media websites. Using the internet, or CDs from the library, you can find most of Bach's music. When you listen to the music, remember that Bach took time to think about each note. Just like an author considers every word that gets penned on paper, so too do musicians think about each note. If you listen to the vast amount of music that Bach produced and the complexity of it, you will be astounded that one man managed to do so much work.

When Bach was sixty-two years old, in the year 1747, he received excellent news. His daughter-in-law was pregnant! She lived in Berlin, the capital of Germany. He knew that he needed to visit her immediately and congratulate her on this wonderful occasion. However, on his way to Berlin, he needed to make a quick pit stop.

The king of Prussia (which is no longer a country, but which later became parts of Germany, and other European countries), King Frederick the Great had invited Bach to play for him. Bach was more than happy to do this. First the King of Poland, and now the King of Prussia! The king wanted Bach to try his new instruments, including an instrument known as the fortepiano. The *fortepiano* was an early version of what we now call the *piano*. The king was so pleased with Bach's playing that he ordered a parade around the city, where Bach would play the organ for all to hear. It was truly a sight to see!

After the performance, Bach went on to his daughter and then returned home to Leipzig. He soon began experiencing eye problems. He was finding it harder and harder to see, something that is common in old age. He had surgery on his eyes, but a doctor who hoped to make him better. However, his eyes only became infected and his condition worsened.

However, even with his eyesight in bad shape, he still continued to compose music. His son-in-law Altnikol helped him write down the music and figure things out. Some of his music was finished before he died, and other pieces were not.

In 1750, when Bach was sixty-five years old, he woke up and could suddenly see better! It seemed like a miracle. For too long, his eyes had been hurt by bright sunlight, but he now found it easier to handle. However, he was happiness was short-lived. That very night, he suffered from a stroke, which can happen when your blood or your brain cells do not get enough oxygen. He was put into bed with a rising temperature, a headache, and nausea. That very night, Johann Sebastian Bach passed away.

Bach was buried in a place called St. John's Cemetery three days later. However, for whatever strange reason, he was buried without a headstone. Soon, the common people forgot that the famous composer Bach was buried there — until a hundred and fifty years later, that is. The cemetery church was then reconstructed, and Bach's bones were moved into a sarcophagus, where his memory could be more easily observed.

In World War II, however, another event rattled Bach's bones. From 1939 to 1945, the world plunged into the most dangerous battle in history. On one side stood the United States, the United Kingdom, the Soviet Union (now Russia), Australia, New Zealand, Brazil, Belgium, Denmark, Greece, the Netherlands, Norway, Poland, France, Yugoslavia, China, and South Africa; these countries were known as the Allied forces. On the other side stood Germany, Italy, Japan, Hungary, Romania, and Bulgaria. World War II featured many bombings between these countries, and Germany was struck several times. During one of the Allied bombing raids, St. John's Church was hit, and so were the remains of Johann Sebastian Bach.

Four years after the war ended, in 1949, Bach's bones were discovered and moved again. Today, you can see a Bach memorial in the church of St. Thomas in Germany, where Bach had often performed with the students in the St. Thomas school.

Chapter 6: The B A C H Motif and Basic Music Theory

When studying Bach, there is something very interesting that we can learn about his name. In German, his name can be spelled out with musical notes on a staff. Here is how:

Firstly, you must understand that on a musical staff, a note is placed on each line. Each line stands for a different note. The notes run from letters A to G, and then repeat. Technically, it is possible to spell out basic words like "DAD" on a staff (first the "D" note, then the "A" note, then the "D" note again). You could essentially turn the word "dad" into a short musical phrase. But there are notes *between* the notes as well, and these other notes come in the form of *sharps* and *flats*. A *sharp* note is higher (sharps are identified by a pound, or hashtag, sign), and a *flat* note is lower (marked by a signal that looks like a curved "b." A note that has no sharp or flat is known as *natural*. So, for example, from lower to higher, here is a list of a few notes.

A sharp (B flat)

B natural
B sharp (C flat)
C natural
C sharp (D flat)

Sharp and *flat* notes can be the same. For example, "A sharp" is higher than "A natural." But "A sharp" is the same thing as "B flat," because "B flat" is lower than "B natural." If there is still confusion, many online websites can clear this subject up.

So, with this in mind, how can a musical staff spell out "BACH" if there is no "H" in the musical alphabet?

Well, things are done a bit differently in Germany. In German, a B flat is called a B, and a B natural is referred to as an H. Since an H has now been added to the musical alphabet, one can spell BACH on a staff by writing the notes:

B flat
A natural
C natural
B natural (H)

Bach realized this during his lifetime, but he did not want to tell anyone. When asked why he did not tell anyone, he said that people might think that he was arrogant. However, people thought it was really cool! His children and his students started to write songs that involved what became known as the "BACH Motif." He is likely one of the only composers that can spell out his name on a musical staff (only in German though).

I'll Be Bach: Legacy of a Composer

It's obvious to see that Bach was an inspiring composer. He clearly accomplished what he set out to do: create music that praised God, and to please the masses. He did more than that, and his name went down in history as one of the most famous and successful composers of all time, if not *the* most famous and successful. Not only did he inspire the common people at church services and city performances, but also his colleagues. Famous musicians, such as Ludwig van Beethoven and Wolfgang Amadeus Mozart, loved Bach's music, and they studied it extensively. They learned from him, and then they created successful music of their own. Bach's music was soon to be known around the globe.

Wolfgang Amadeus Mozart, a big name from the classical music era, was born six years after Bach died, but he was still one of Bach's biggest fans. Mozart visited the St. Thomas School, where Bach used to teach, fell onto his knees and held a bunch of music sheets in his hands. It is said that Mozart did not rise until he had thoroughly studied all of the music. Mozart always claimed that much could be learned from Bach, and he was absolutely right.

In the early 1800s, a man named Johann Nikolaus Forkel wrote a biography about Bach that was insanely popular. Even though it was over fifty years after the death of Johann Sebastian Bach, it did help spread the legacy of the acclaimed composer and tell people why Bach was so important. Much of the music in the Classical Era derived from music in the Baroque Era pioneered by Bach.

To understand Bach, and to comprehend why he is so important to the world of music, we have to understand his history. We have to understand his world and his culture. We have to see where he traveled, know why he wrote the music that he did, and feel his frustrations and his joys. There is a reason that "history" has the word "story" in it. Everyone has a story, and the life of Johann Sebastian Bach is a unique one. His music changed the world forever.

Perhaps now, hundreds of years after Bach walked the rich hills of Germany and put ink to paper, it is difficult for us to immediately see what effect he had. It is important to remember, however, that at the time, many people looked up to Bach like many students look up to musical celebrities now. Many people were, and still are, inspired by the great Johann Sebastian Bach. He was not successful just because he was talented; plenty of people around the globe are talented. He was successful because he was willing to try new things, and write down music that no one had written down before. He changed the notes on a paper, and from there he changed the world.

Even though the Baroque Period ended in the same year that he fatefully died, his musical legacy was carried out by his successors. Men like Beethoven and Mozart wrote music after being inspired by him.

Today, people say that if you want to be an author, you have to read, read, read. Read all sorts of books. If you want to write medieval fantasy, you have to read *everything* from romance to history to thriller to horror. The same goes for music. If you want to be a successful musician, you have to get your hands wet. You have to listen and listen and listen, and write and write and write. Practice makes perfect, and as the saying goes, "The tree of knowledge is watered by the bitter tears of experience." Bach made sure that he explored music; he studied music from across the globe, especially French and Italian. And from there, he paved his own path, inspiring many other musicians after him to do the same.